EASTER EGGS

SHADING ACTIVITY BOOK

Thank you for purchasing this activity/practice book. I hope that you and your child will enjoy it.

If you enjoyed it, please visit my store for new apparitions.

Feedback and suggestions are always appreciated. Please leave a review if you can so I can improve this book or make new ones.

This book is for everyone who wants to get good at shading

- Shade the eggs the way you desire to create various designs or forms with graphite pencils. Use multiple tones to add volume to the drawing and limit yourself to only an HB and a 2B pencil.

-If you want to connect some lines left unconnected for various shading techniques, you can do so.

-You can leave the greyscale design as it is or shade over it to obtain a darker tone(difficult for young children).

-This book was created as a family activity book. Children and parents can benefit both from it.

-After shading the egg on both sides of the paper, you or your child can cut it out, or you can keep it in the book and try obtaining other output with the same design existing on the backside of the same sheet.

-After finishing all the eggs or a number you desire, cut them out, string them, and decorate the child's room, Easter dinner table, or give them as gifts to grandparents, teachers, or friends if you will.

Note for parents:

When giving this book to children between 4 - 8 years old, supervise and give directions. They may find shading techniques difficult and tedious. Younger children without hand-eye coordination skills will enjoy colour more than a dull black pencil. Younger children will colour flat with no variation in tones, so give them coloured pencils so they will enjoy the book too.

Please let your child know that if he needs help you will be there for them.

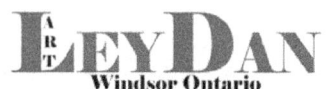

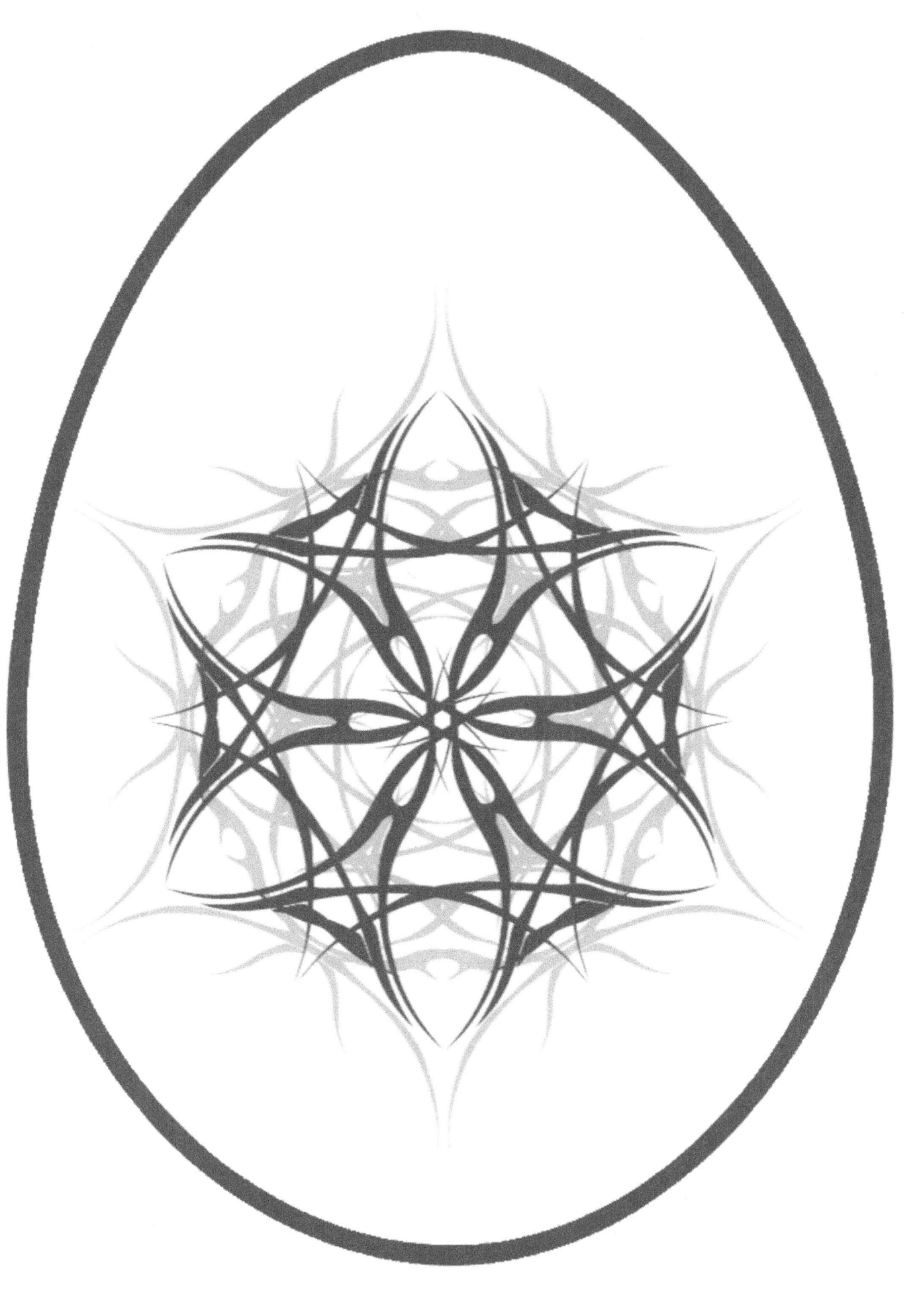

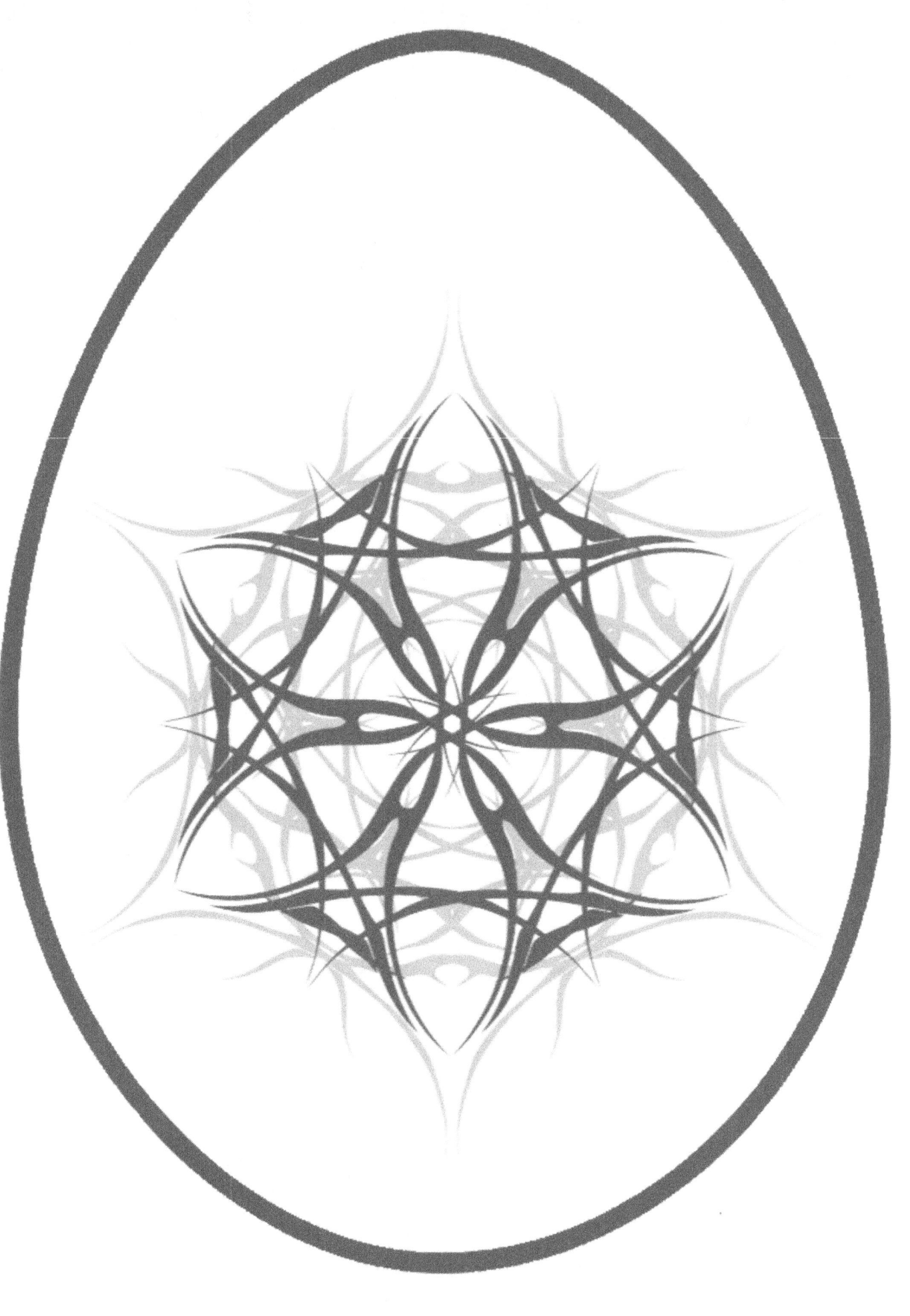

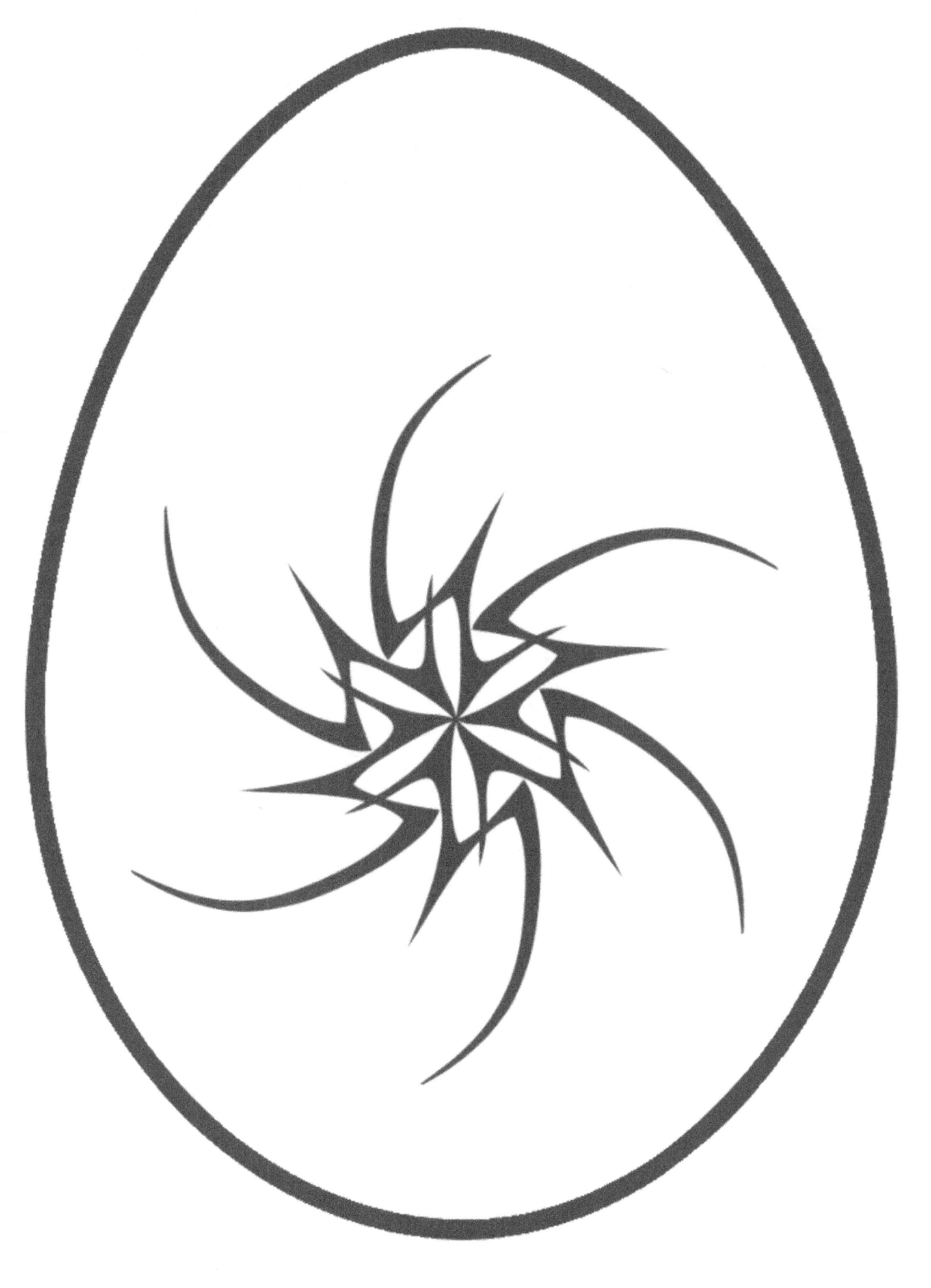

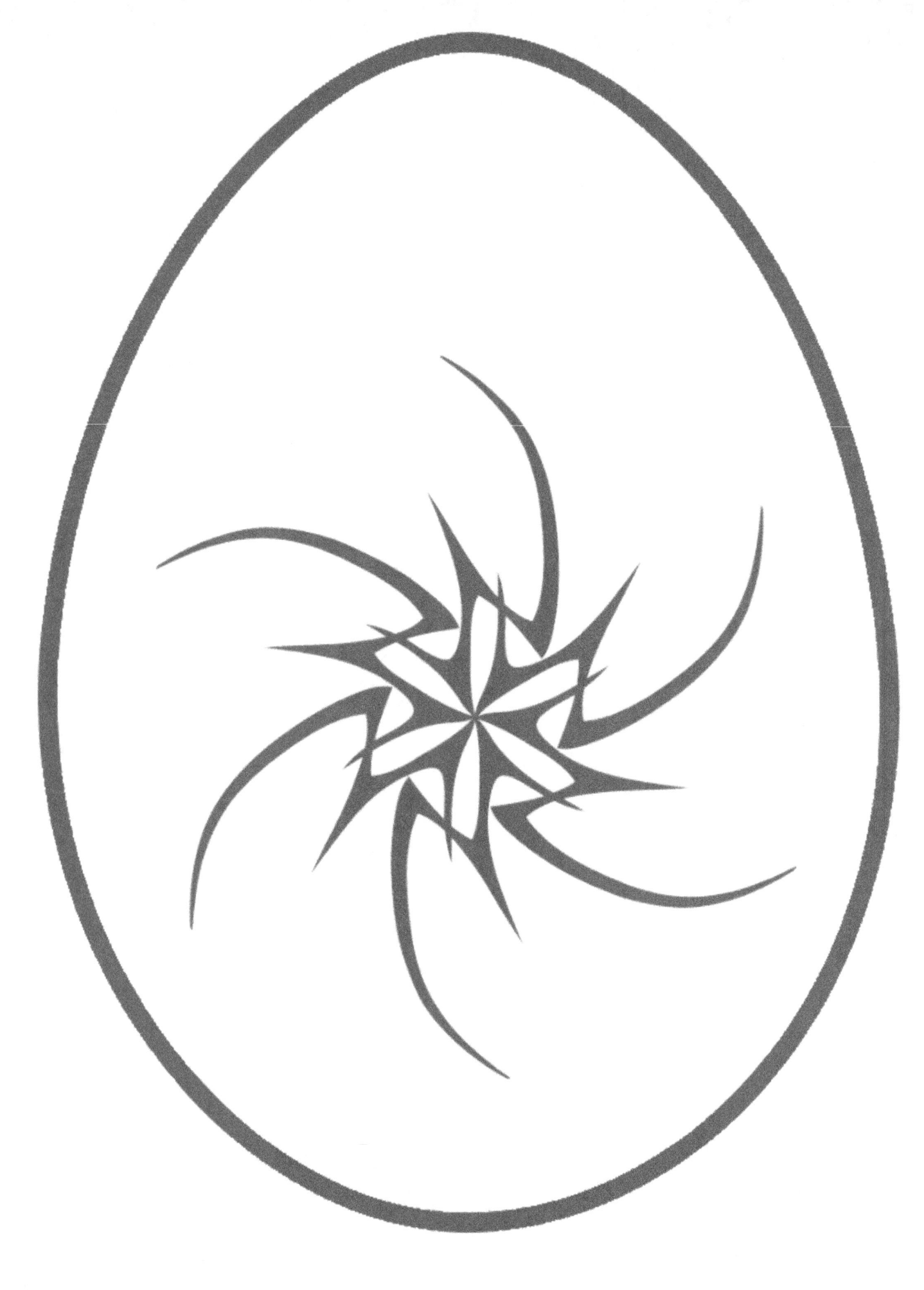

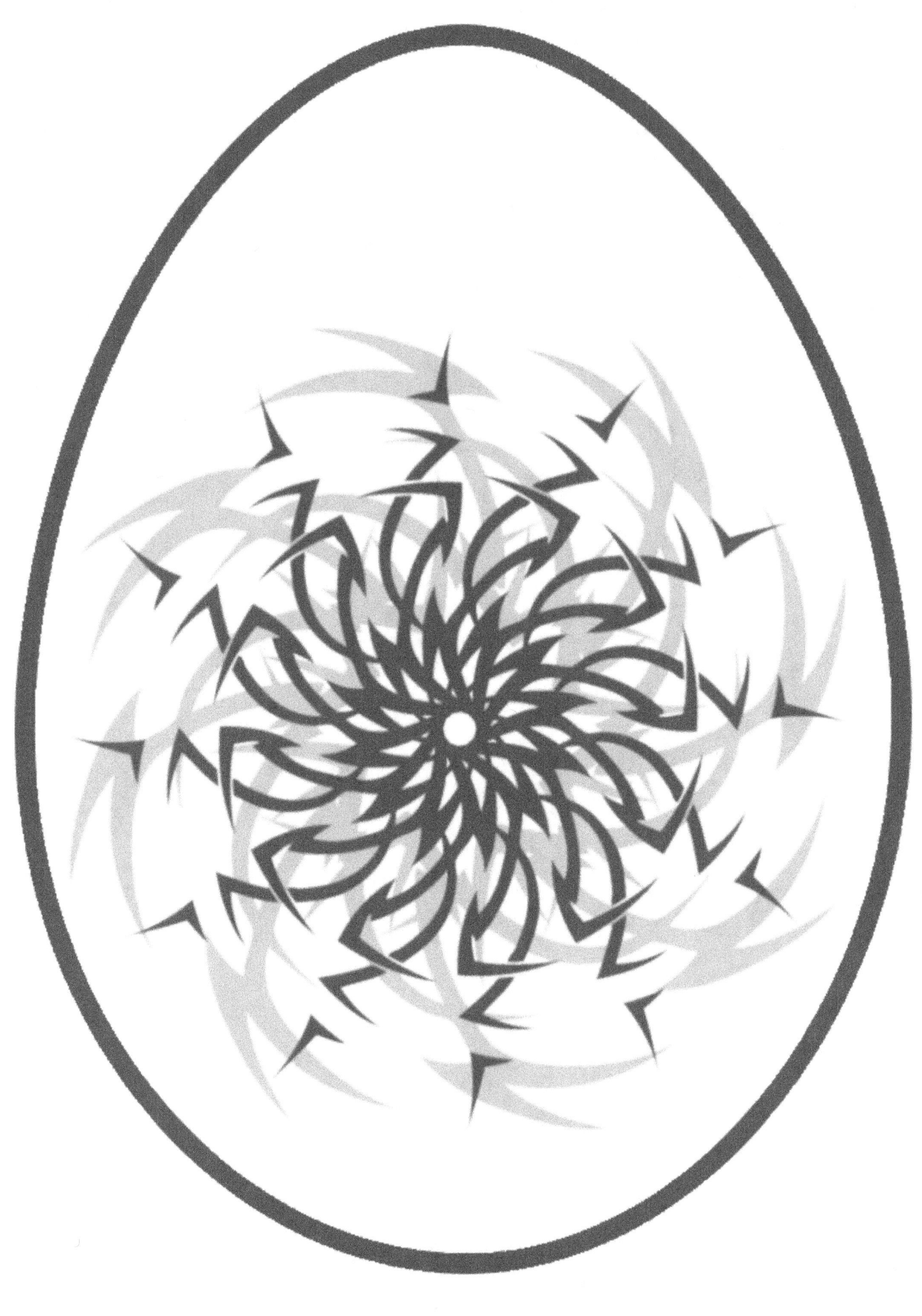

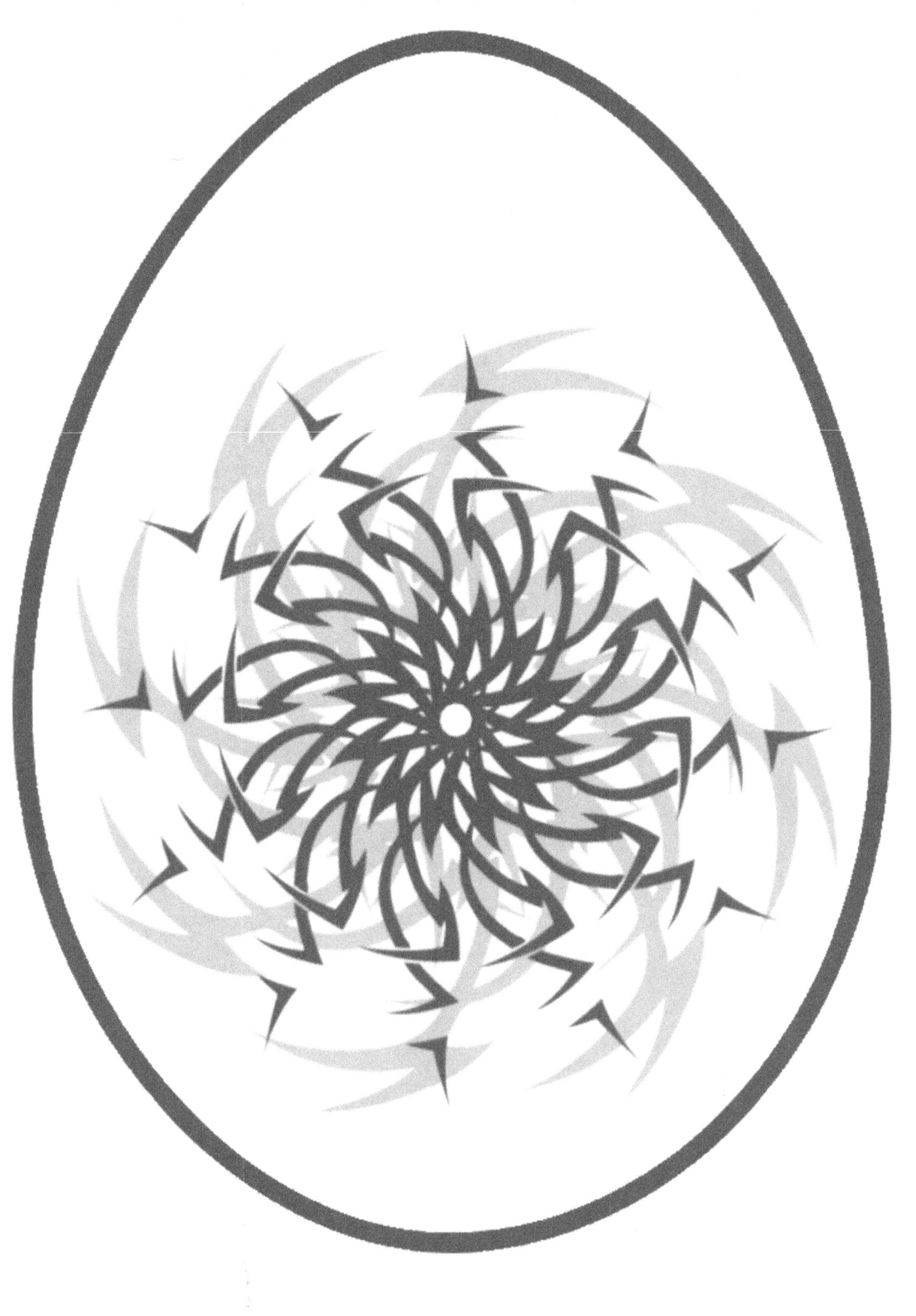

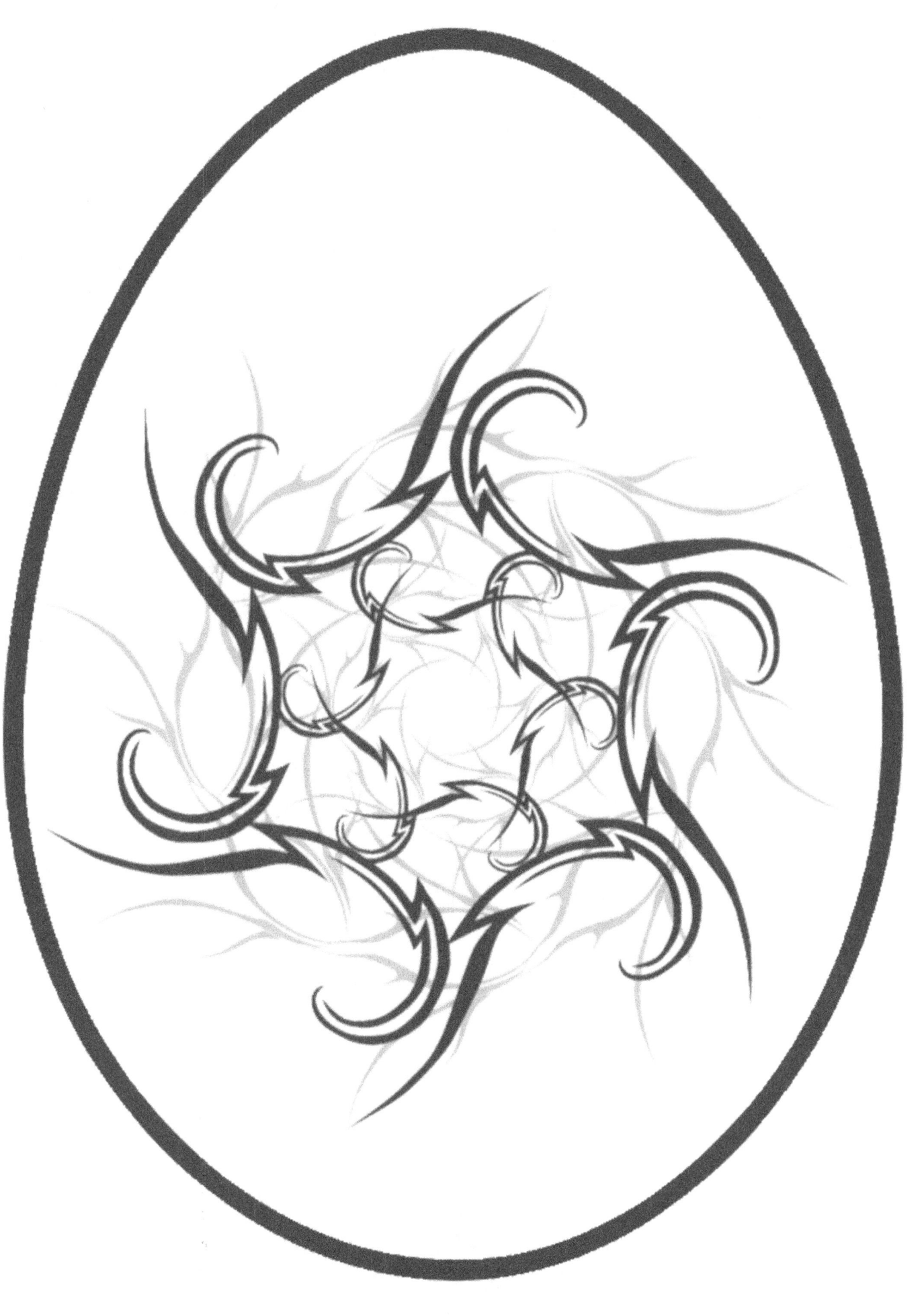

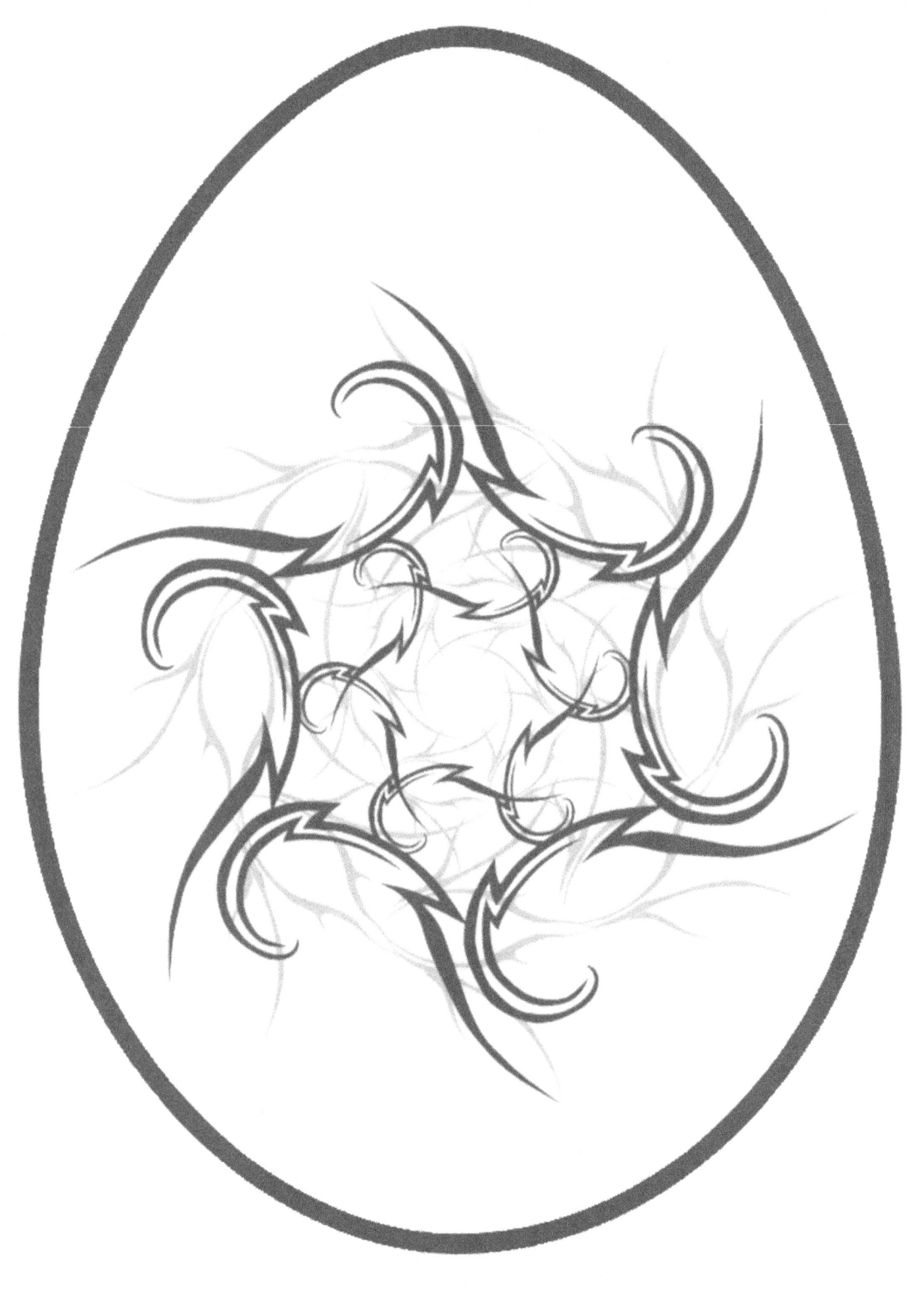

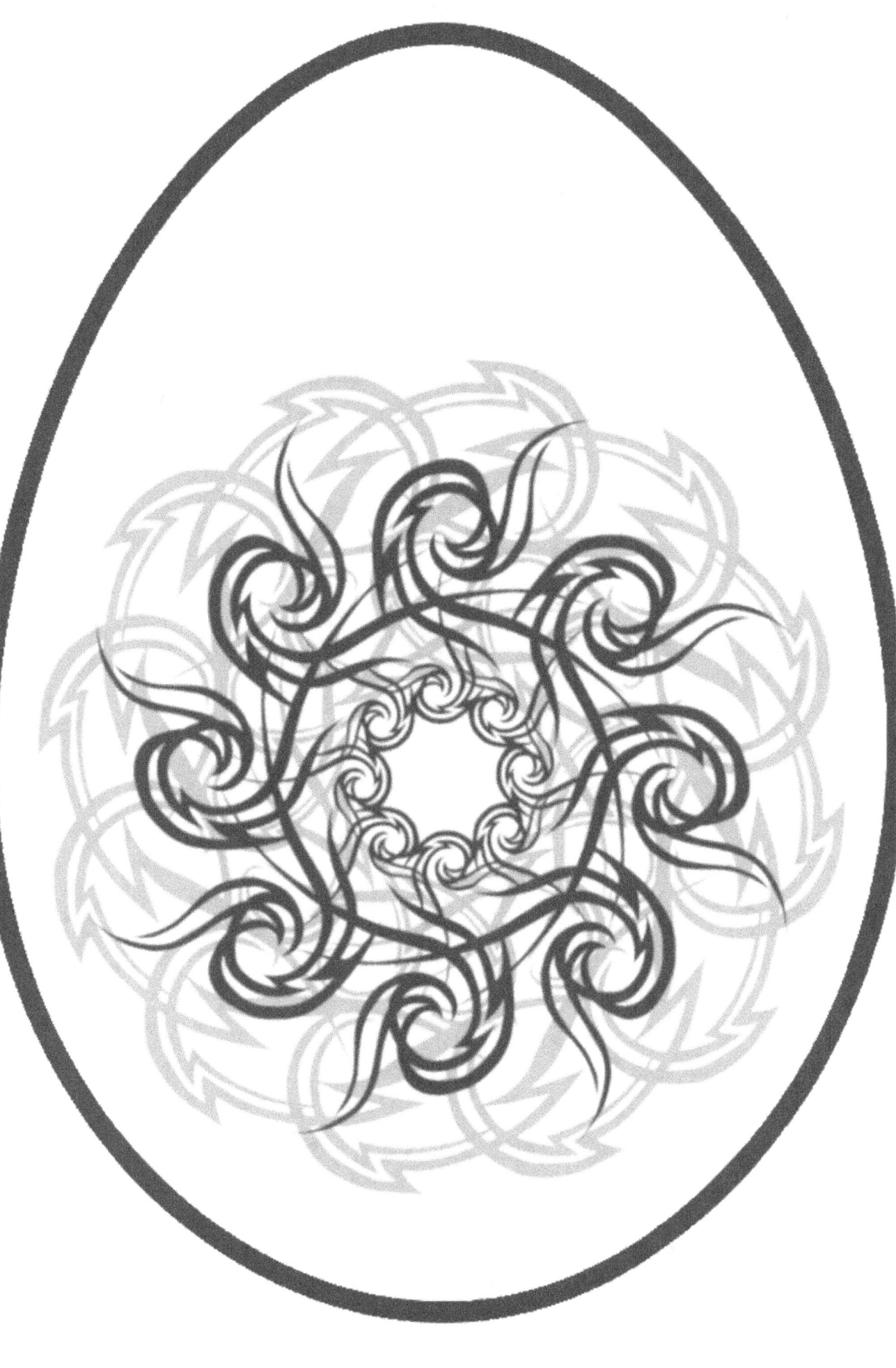

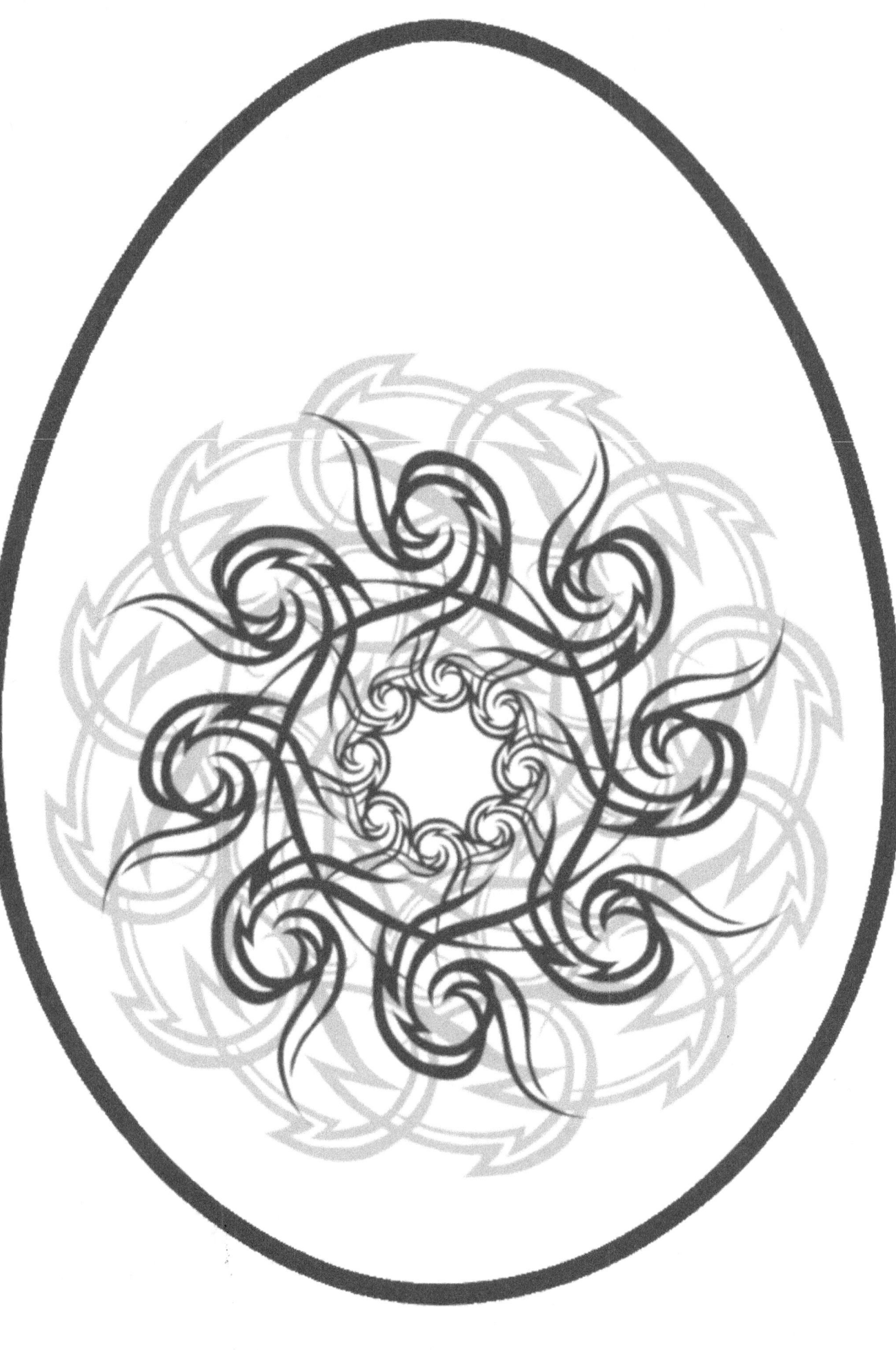

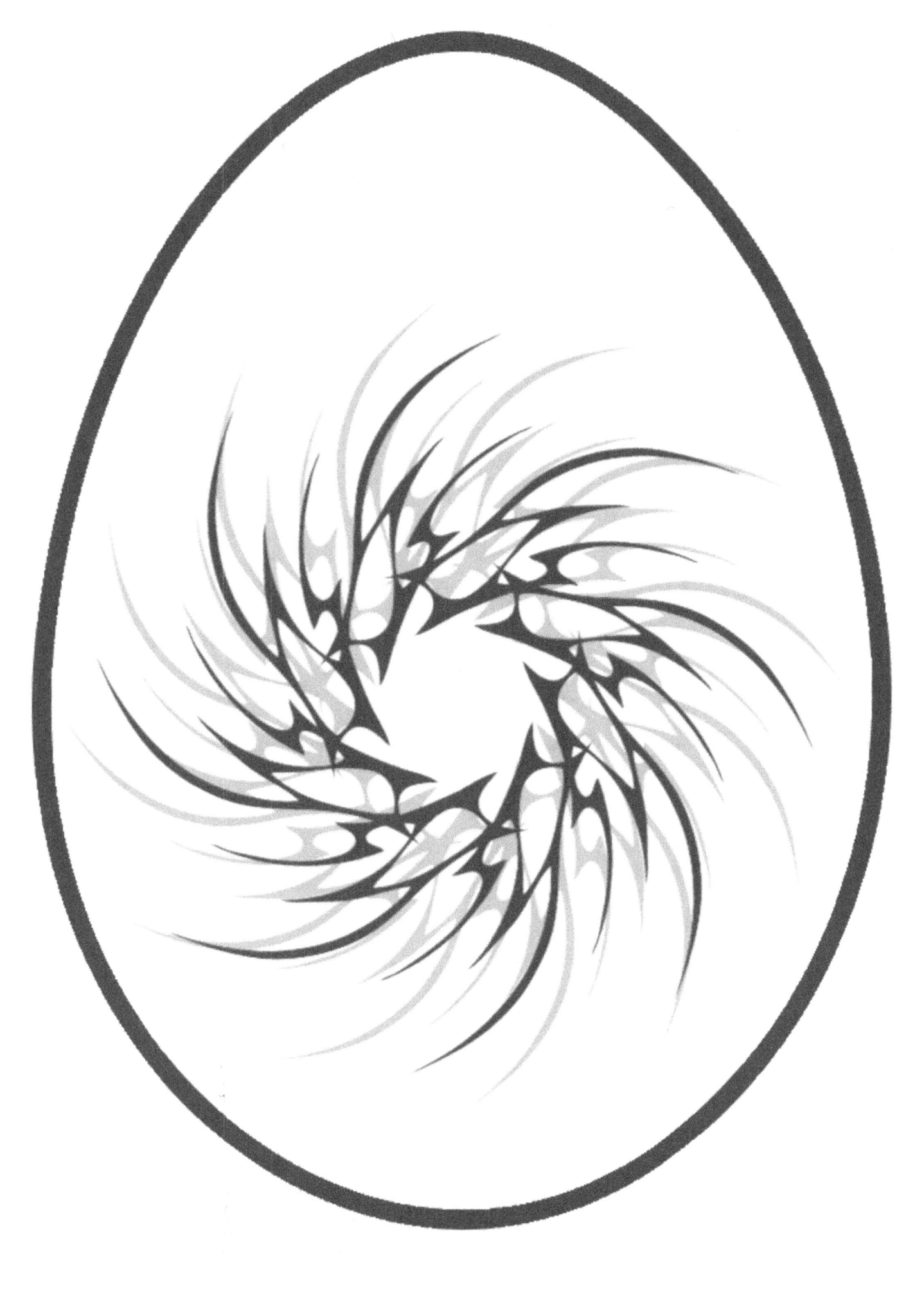

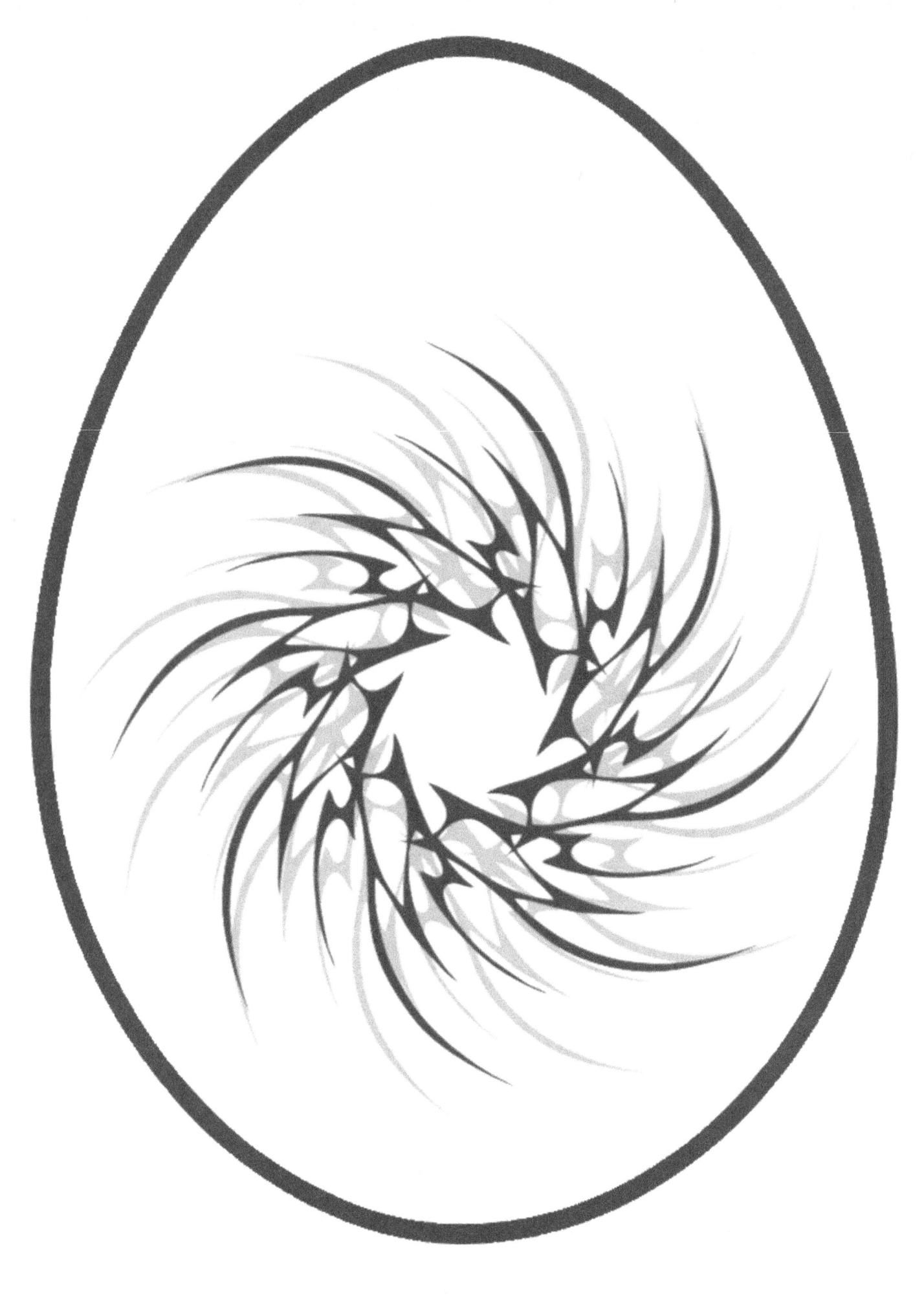

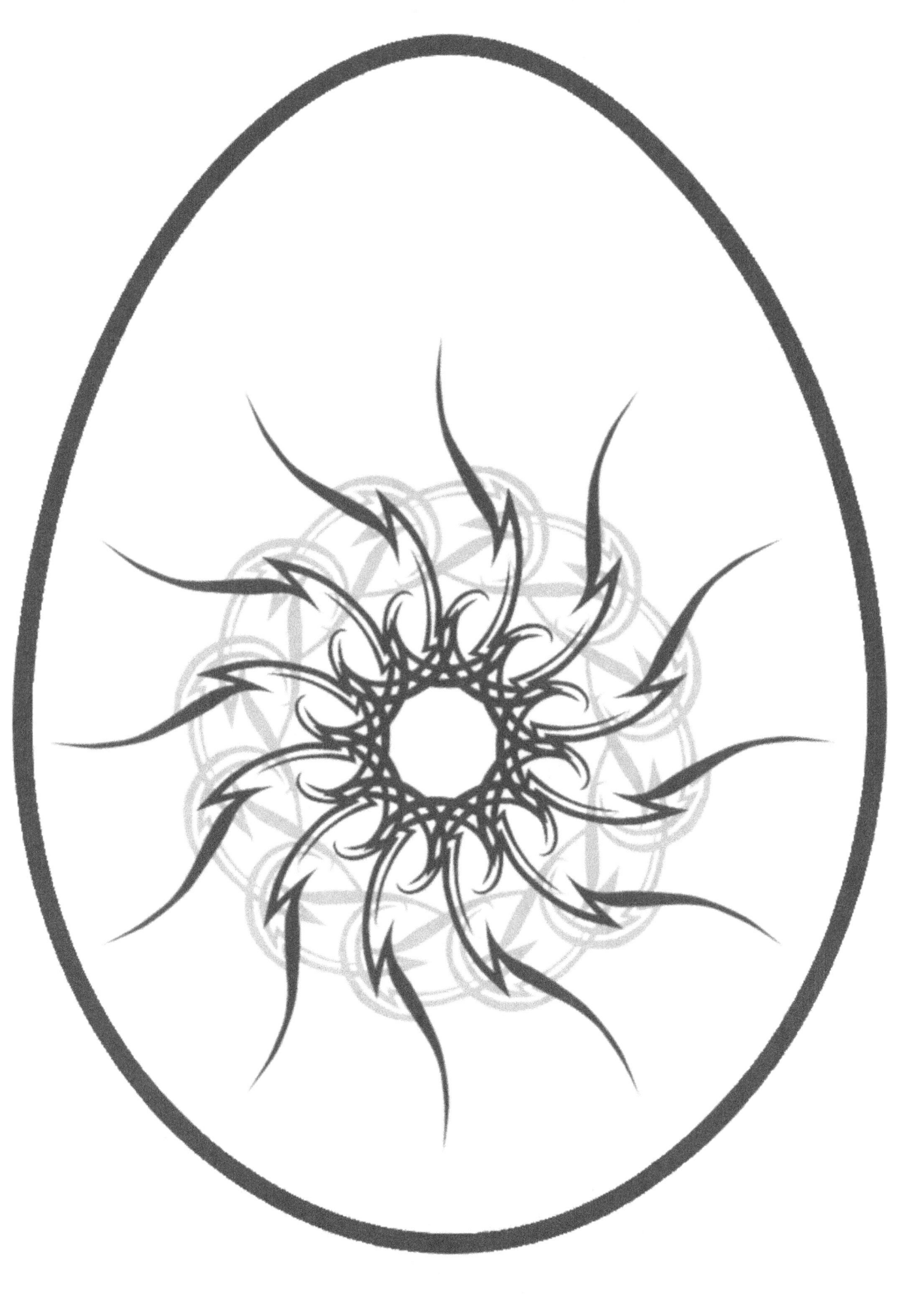

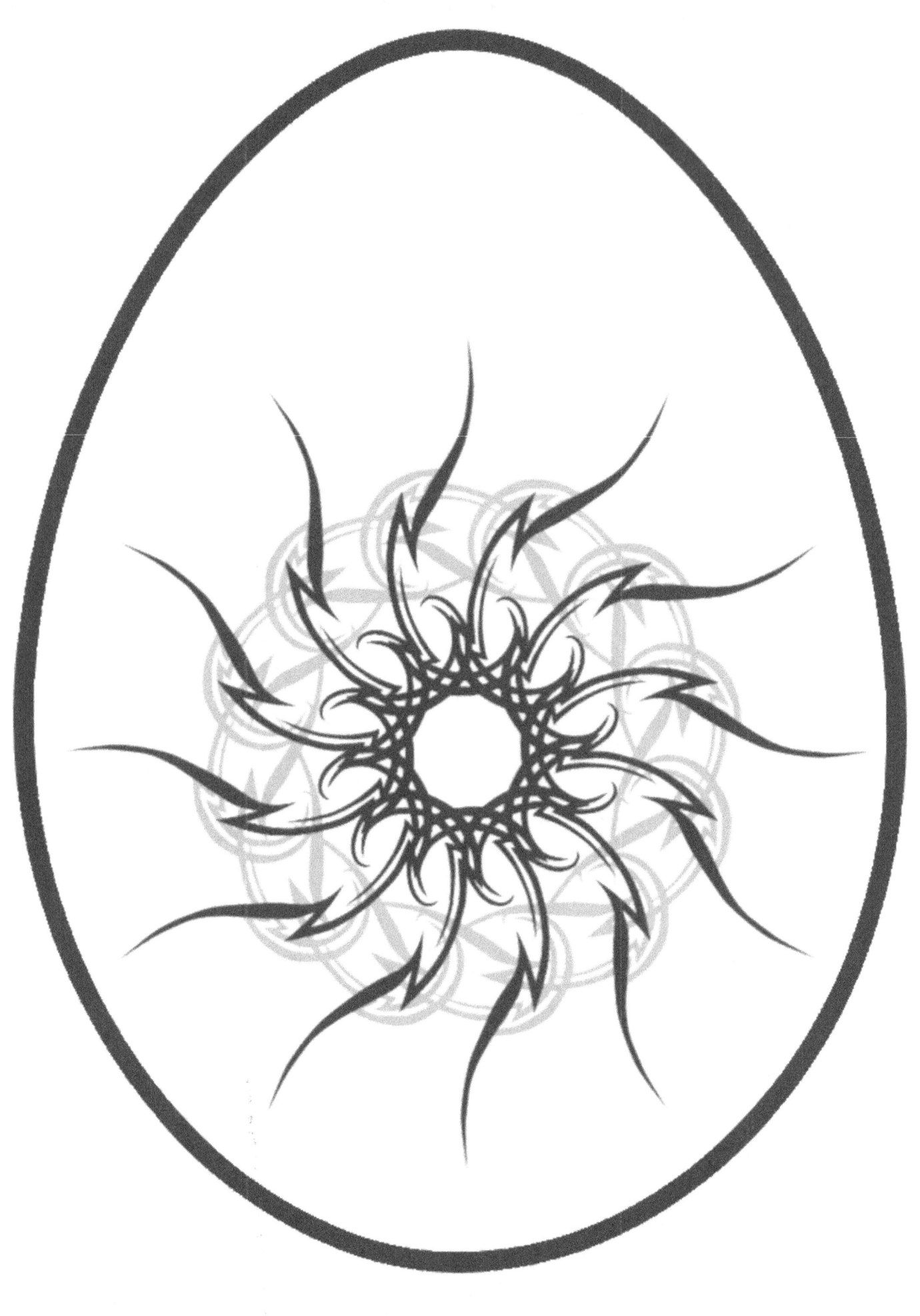

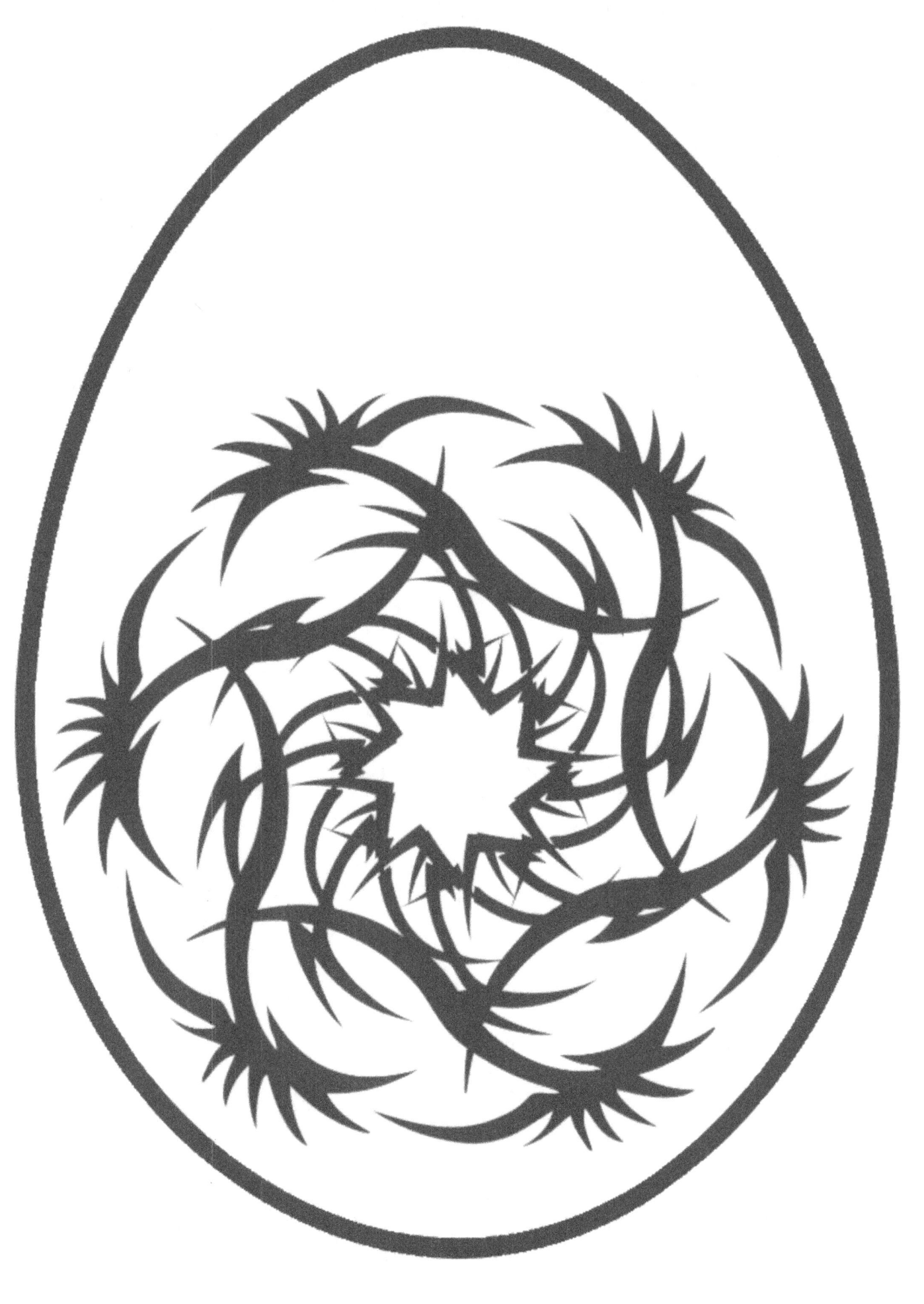

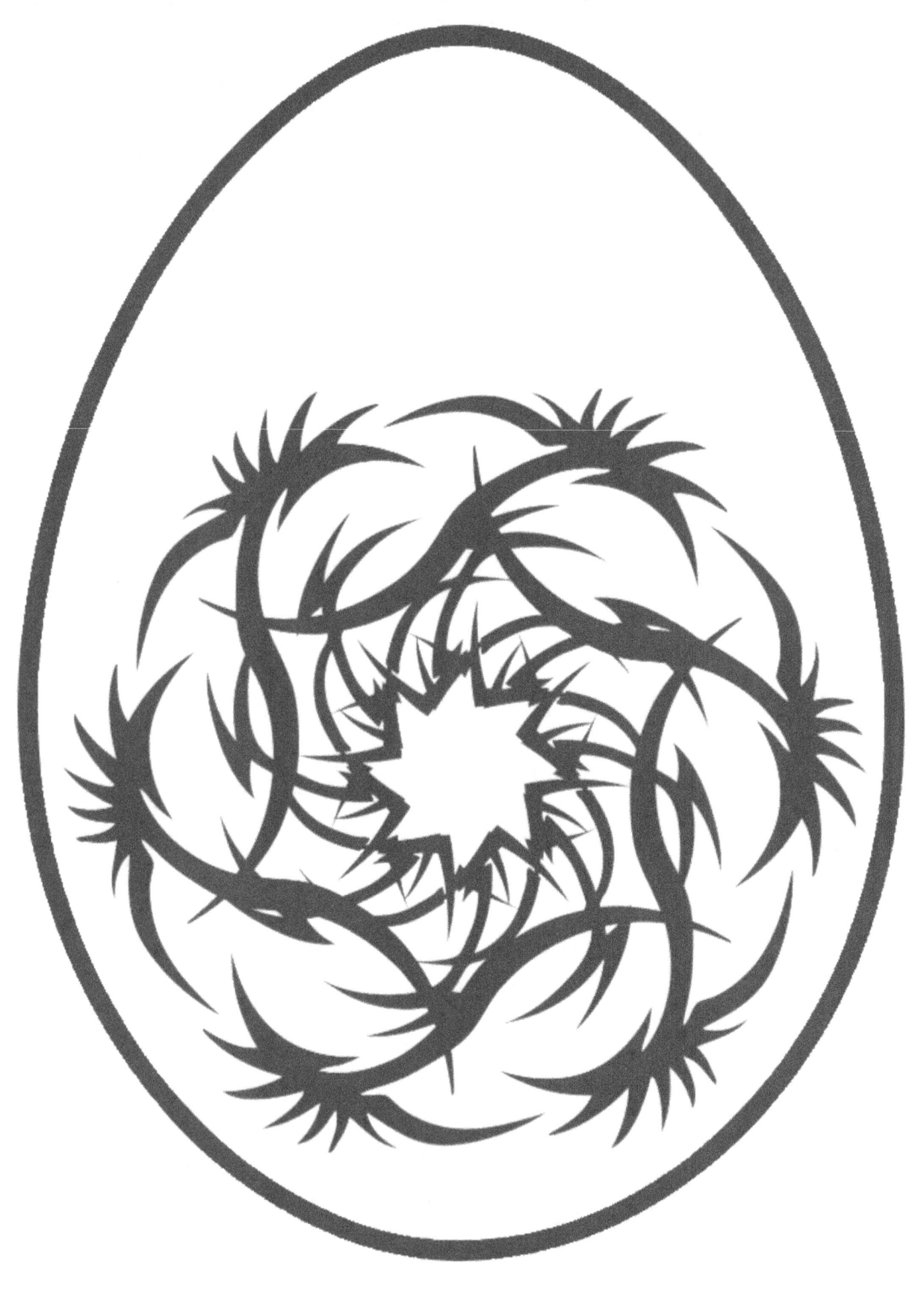

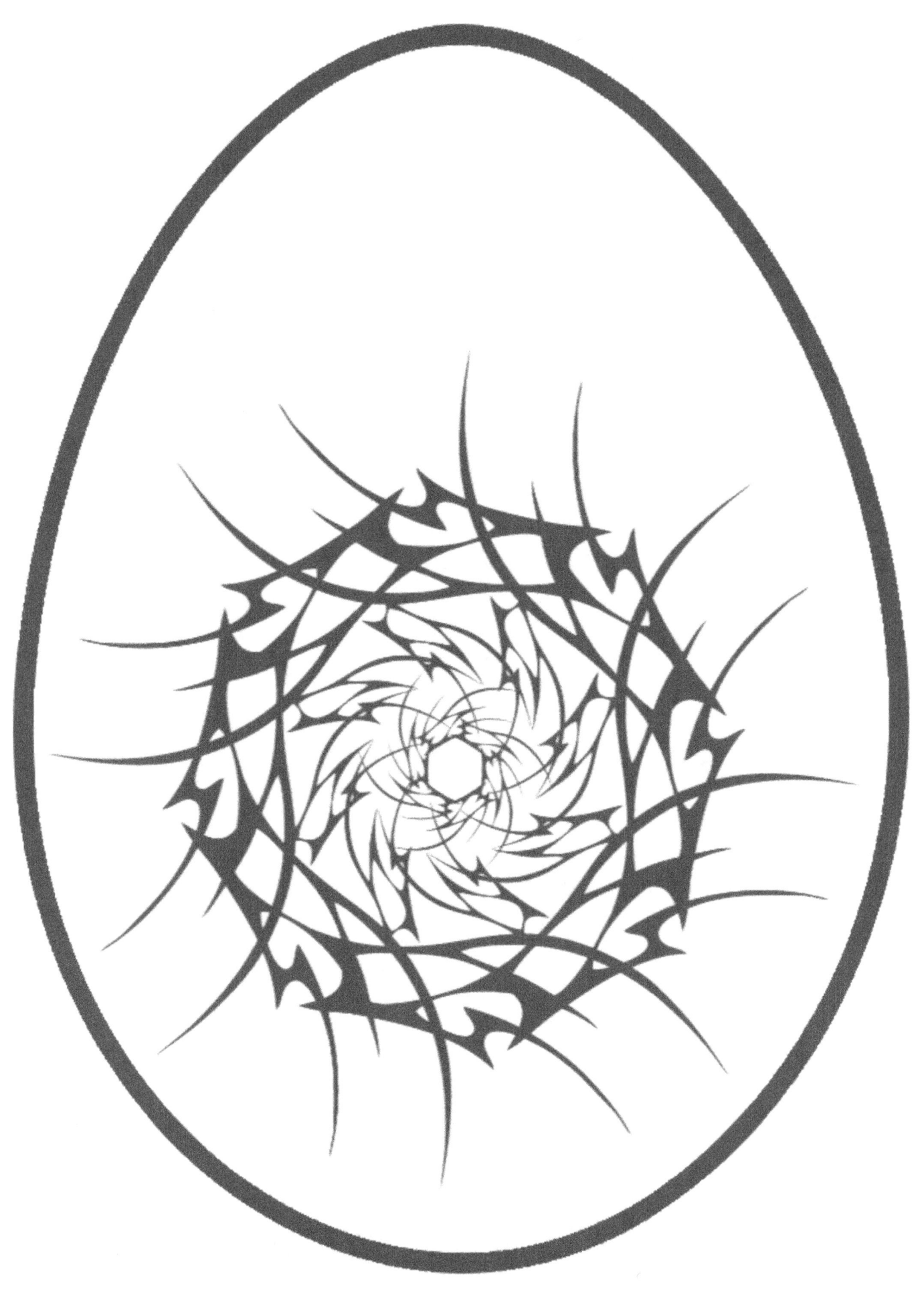

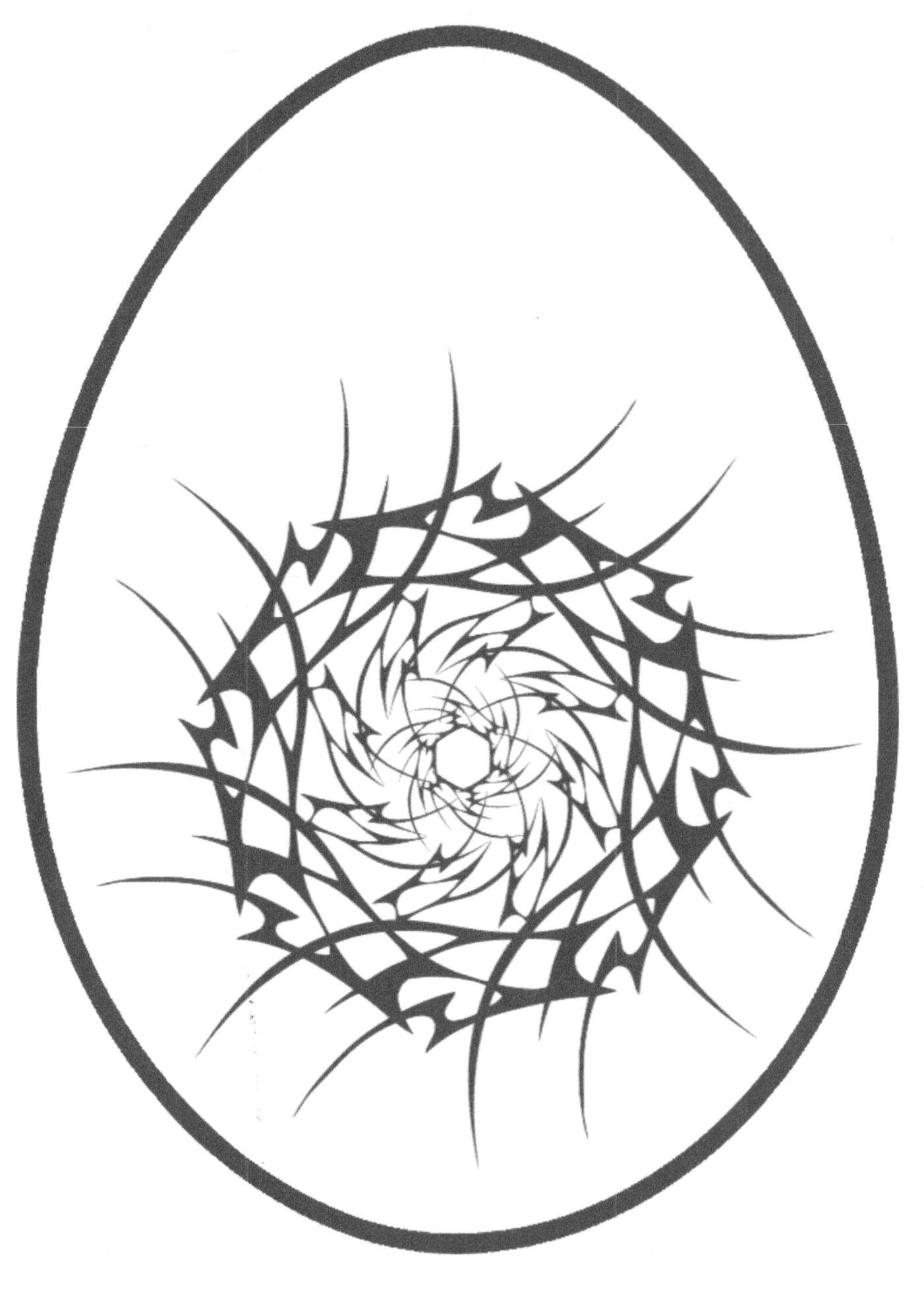

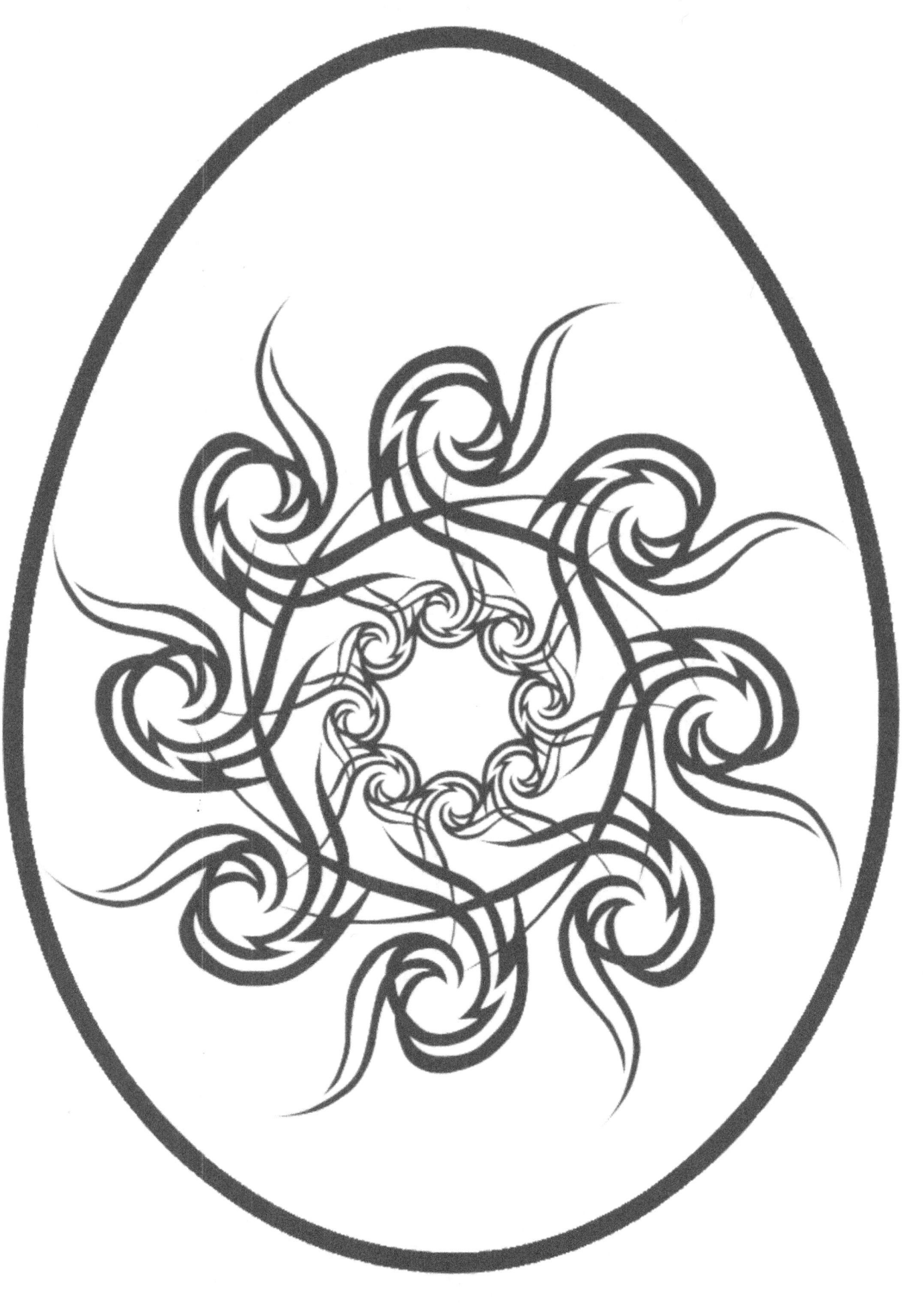

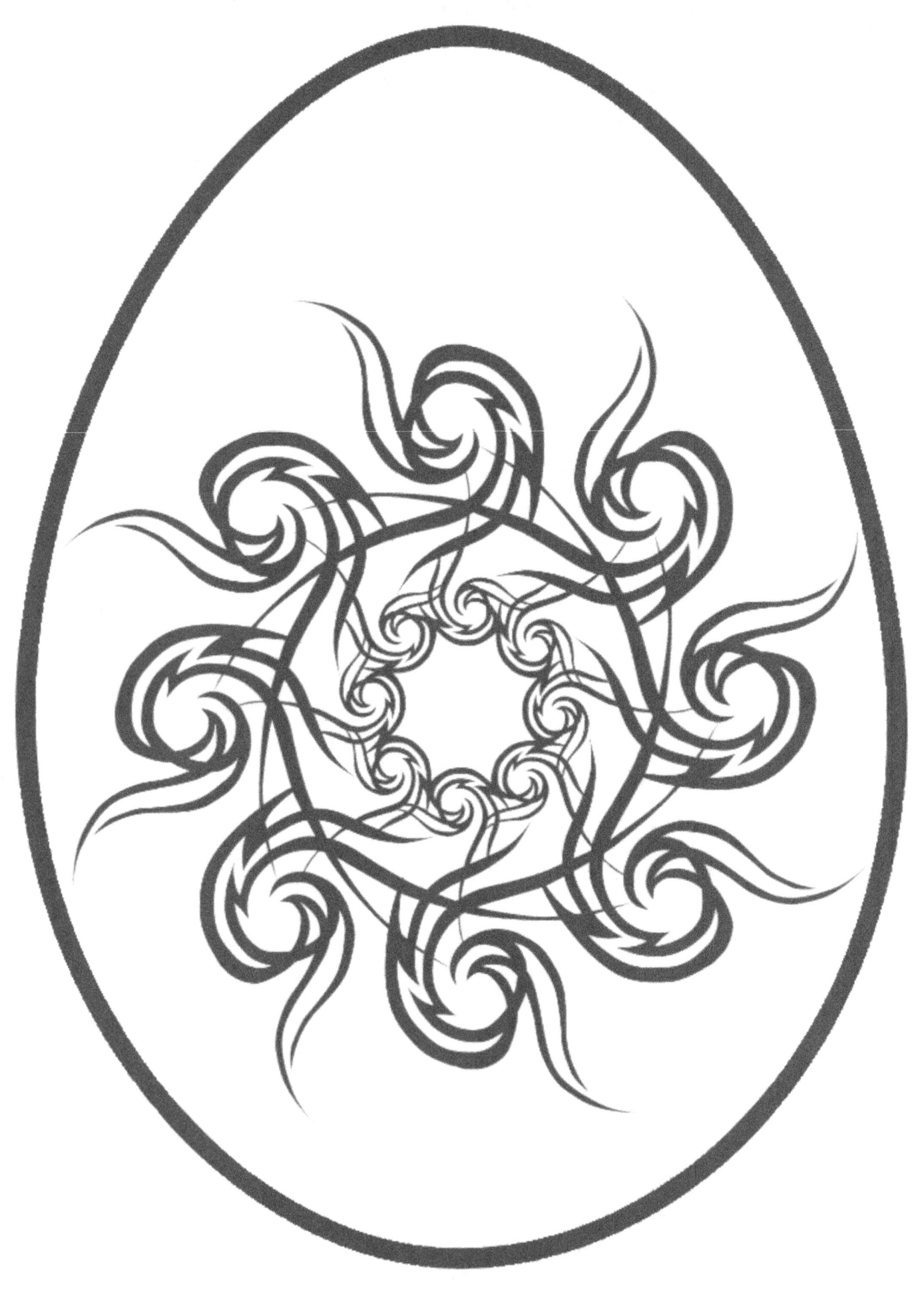

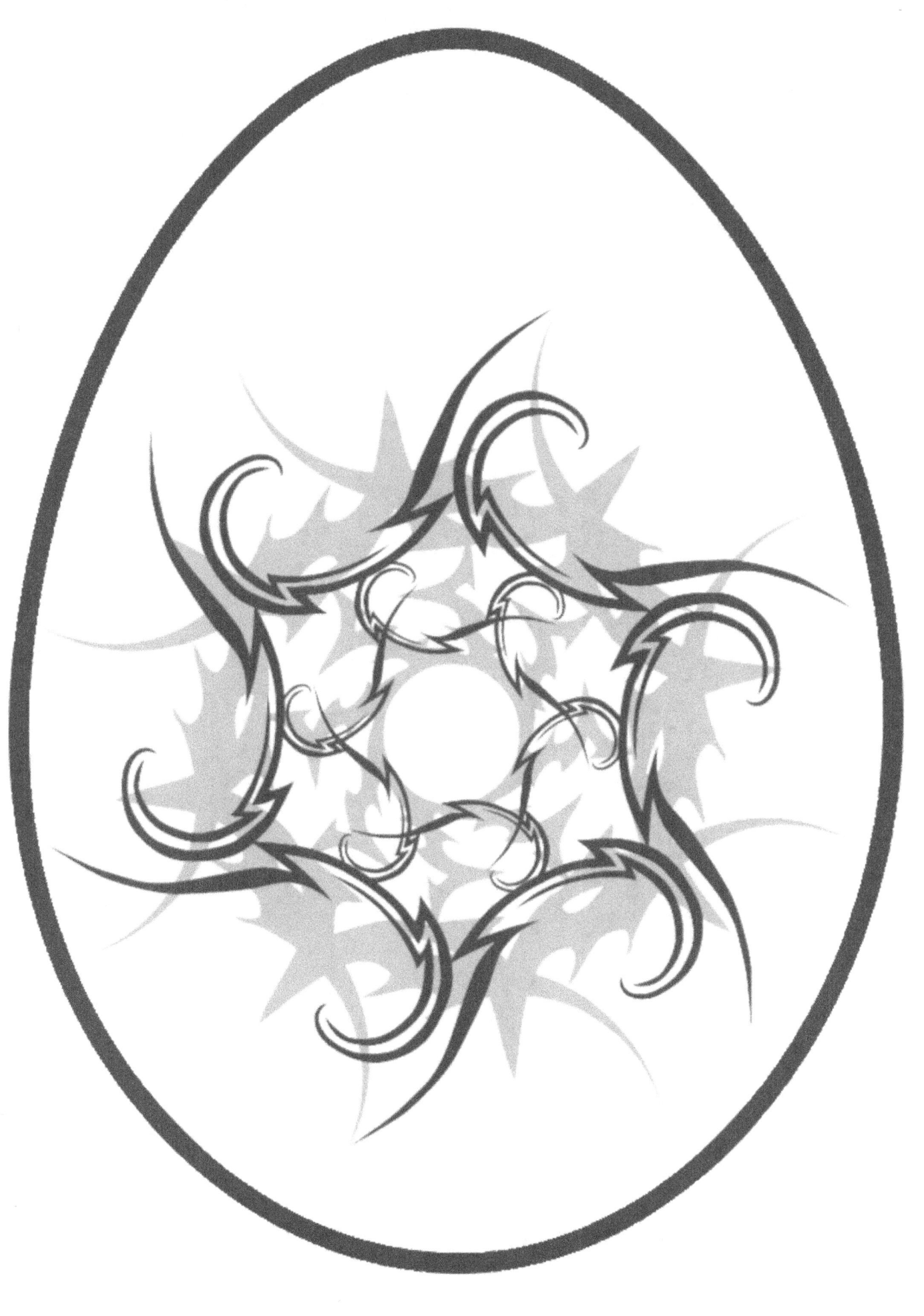

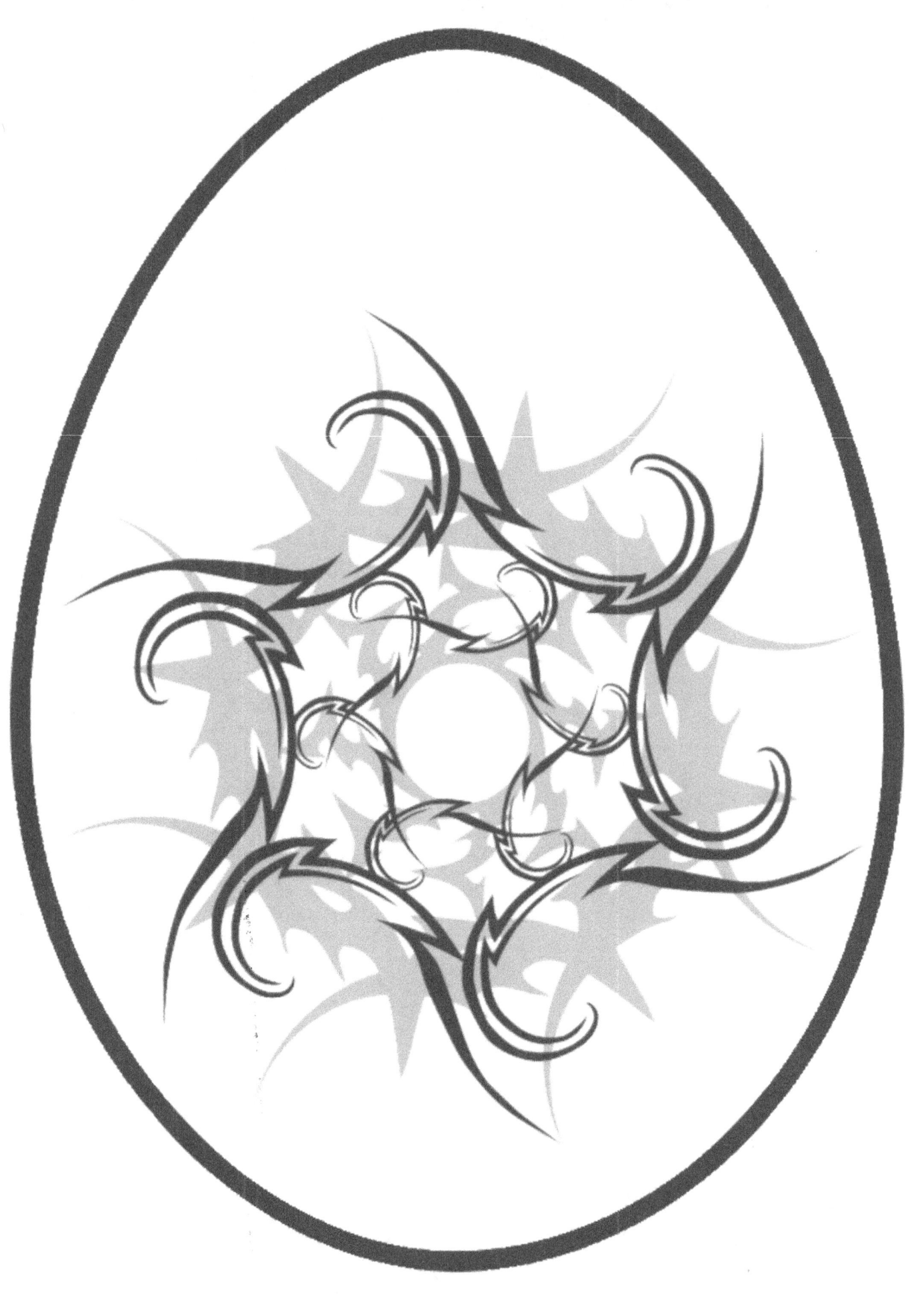

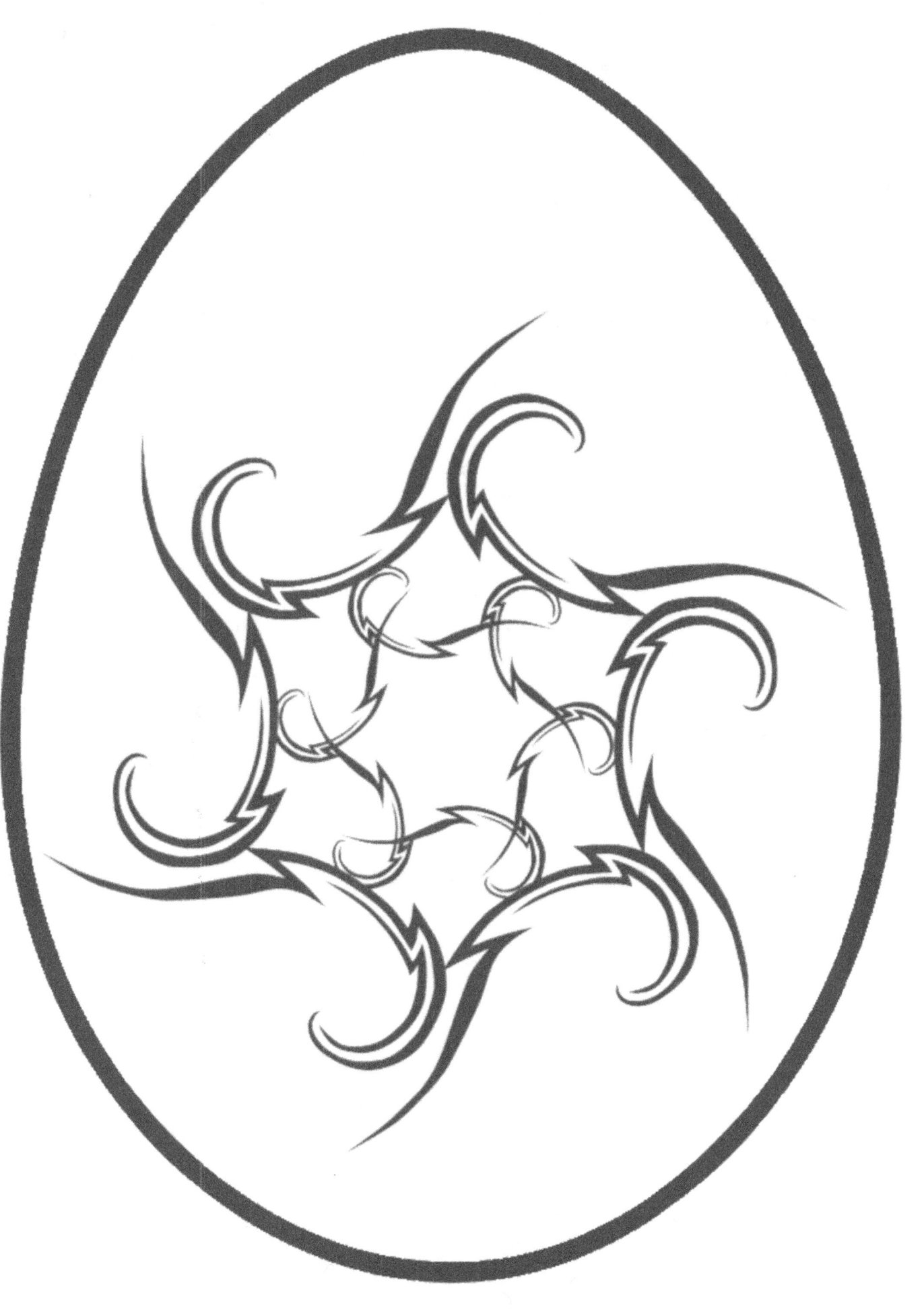

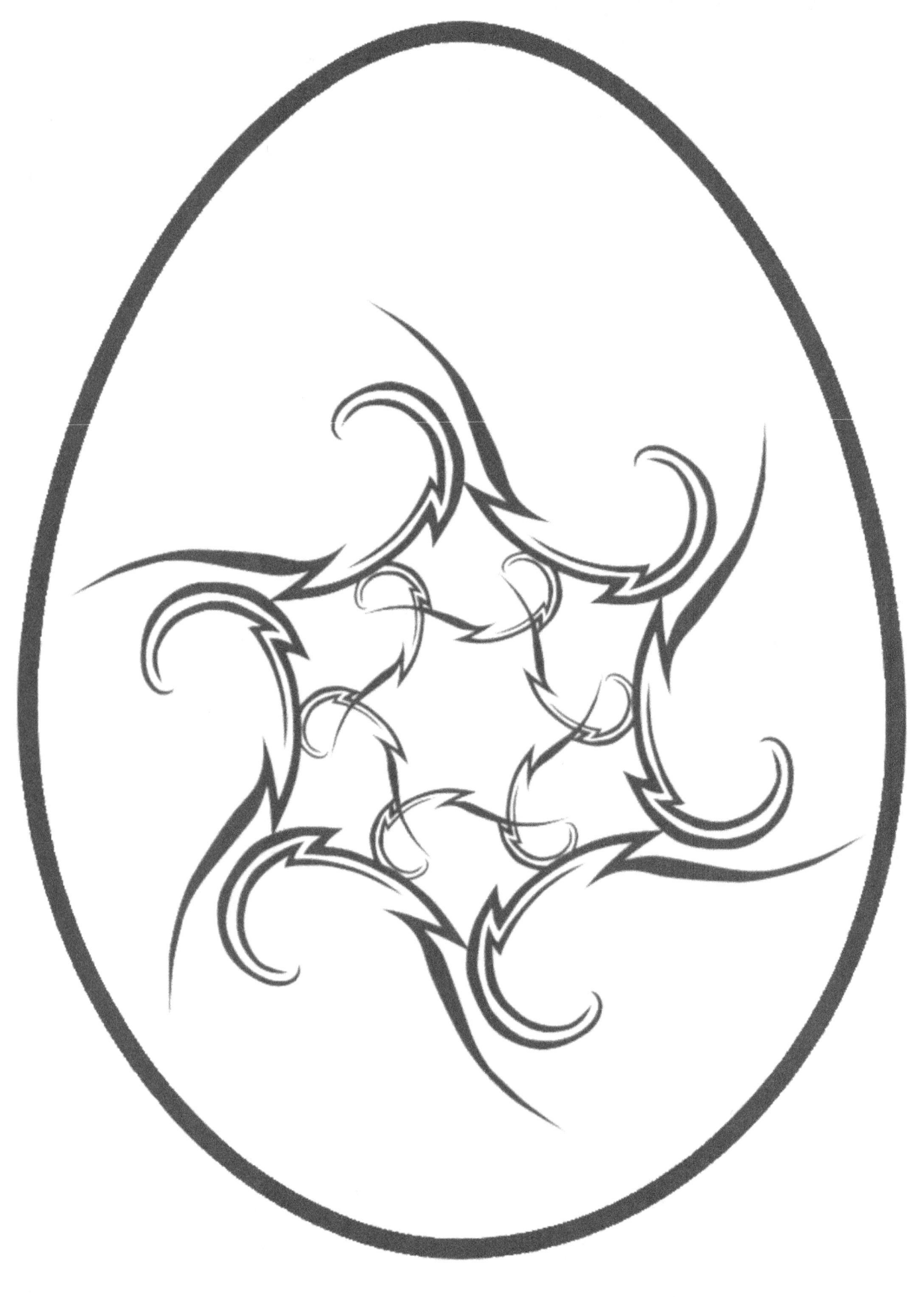

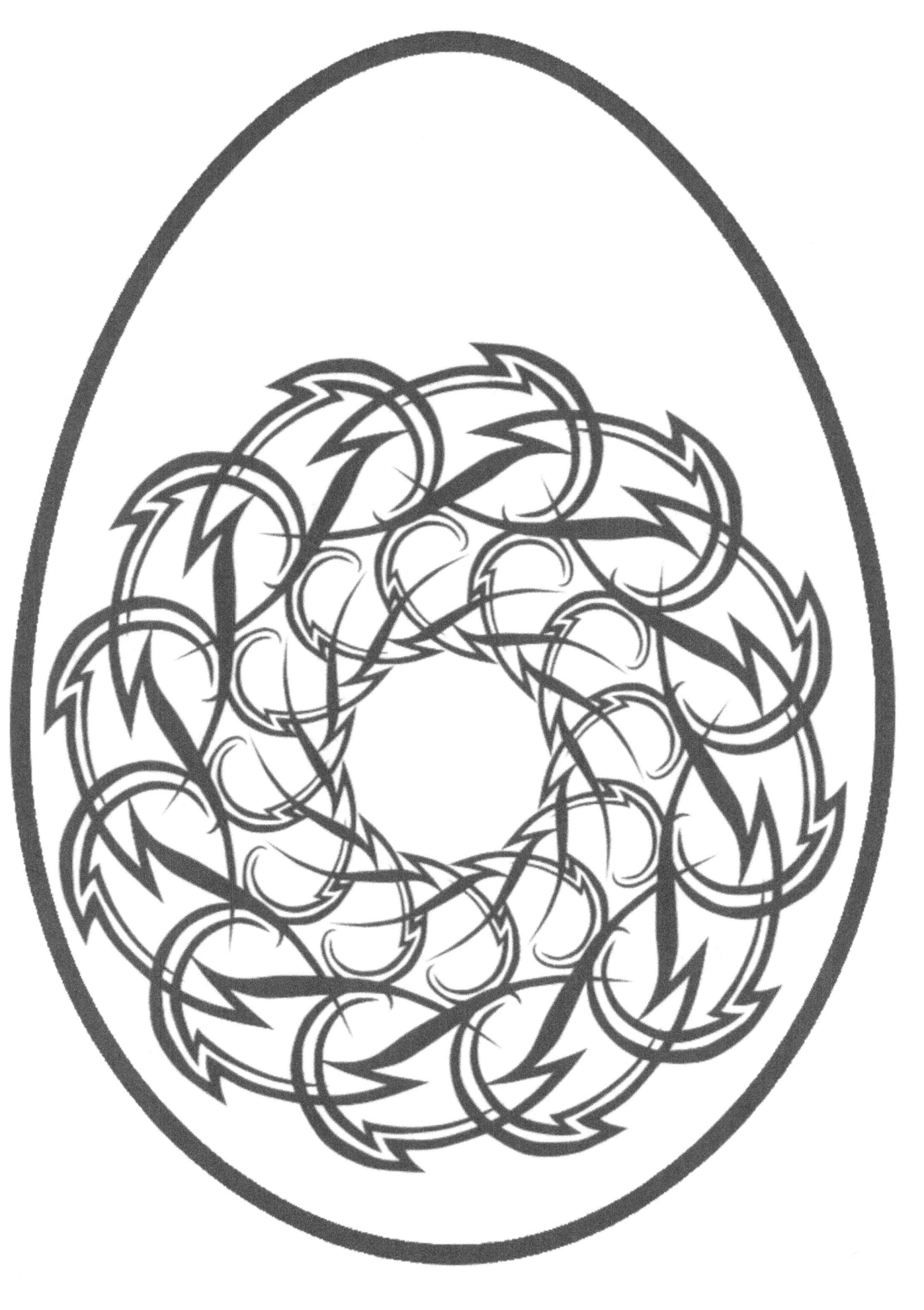

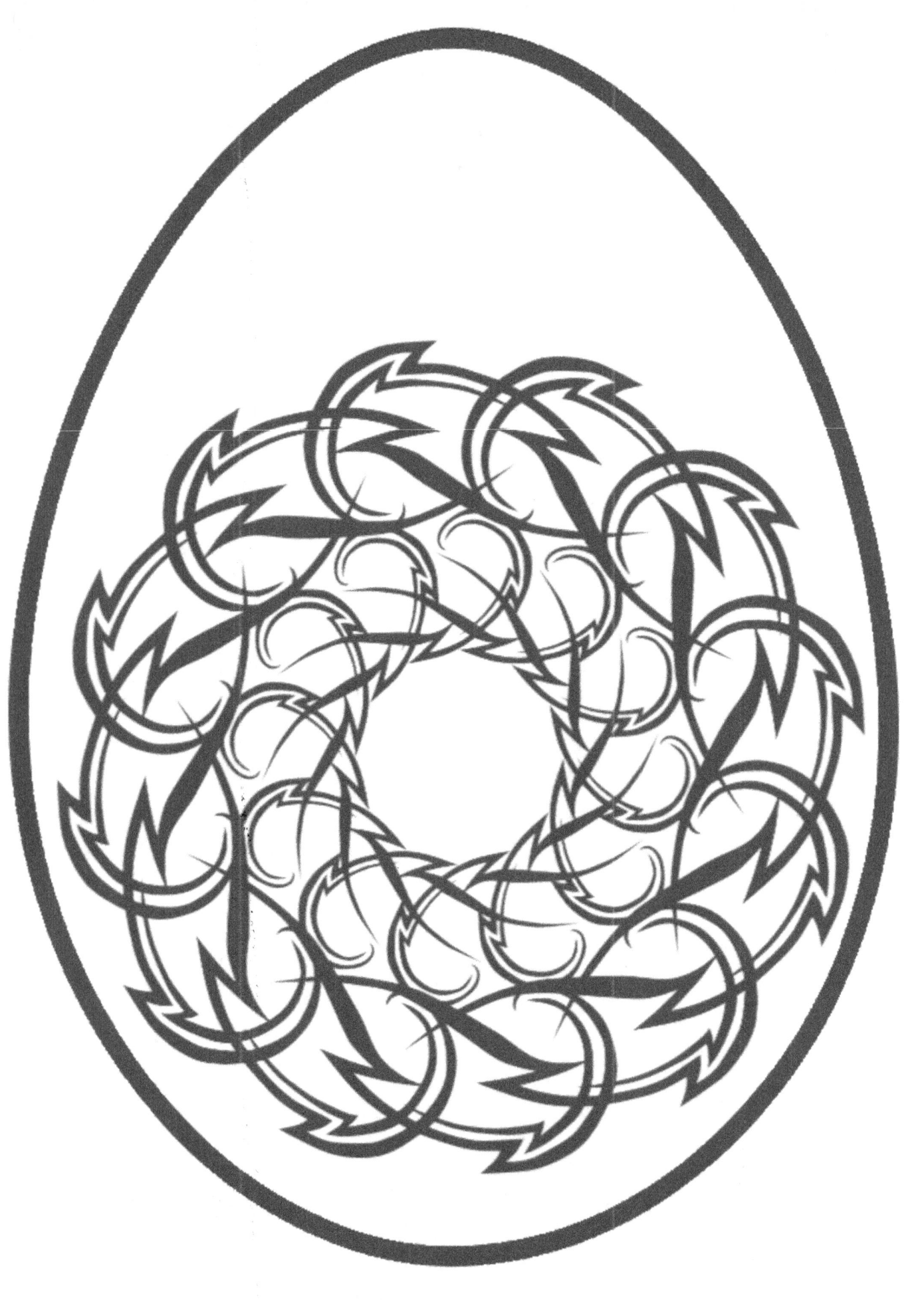

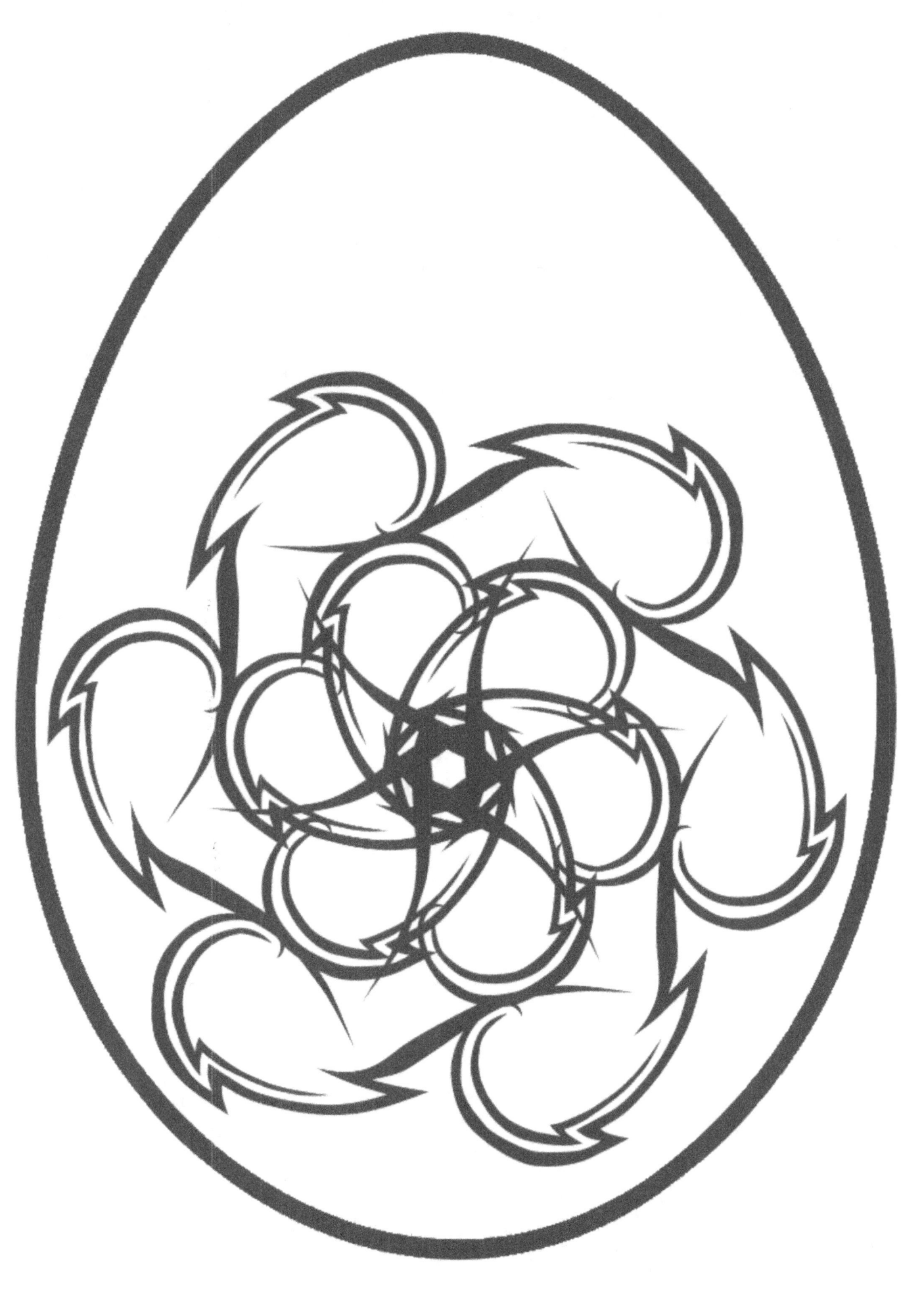

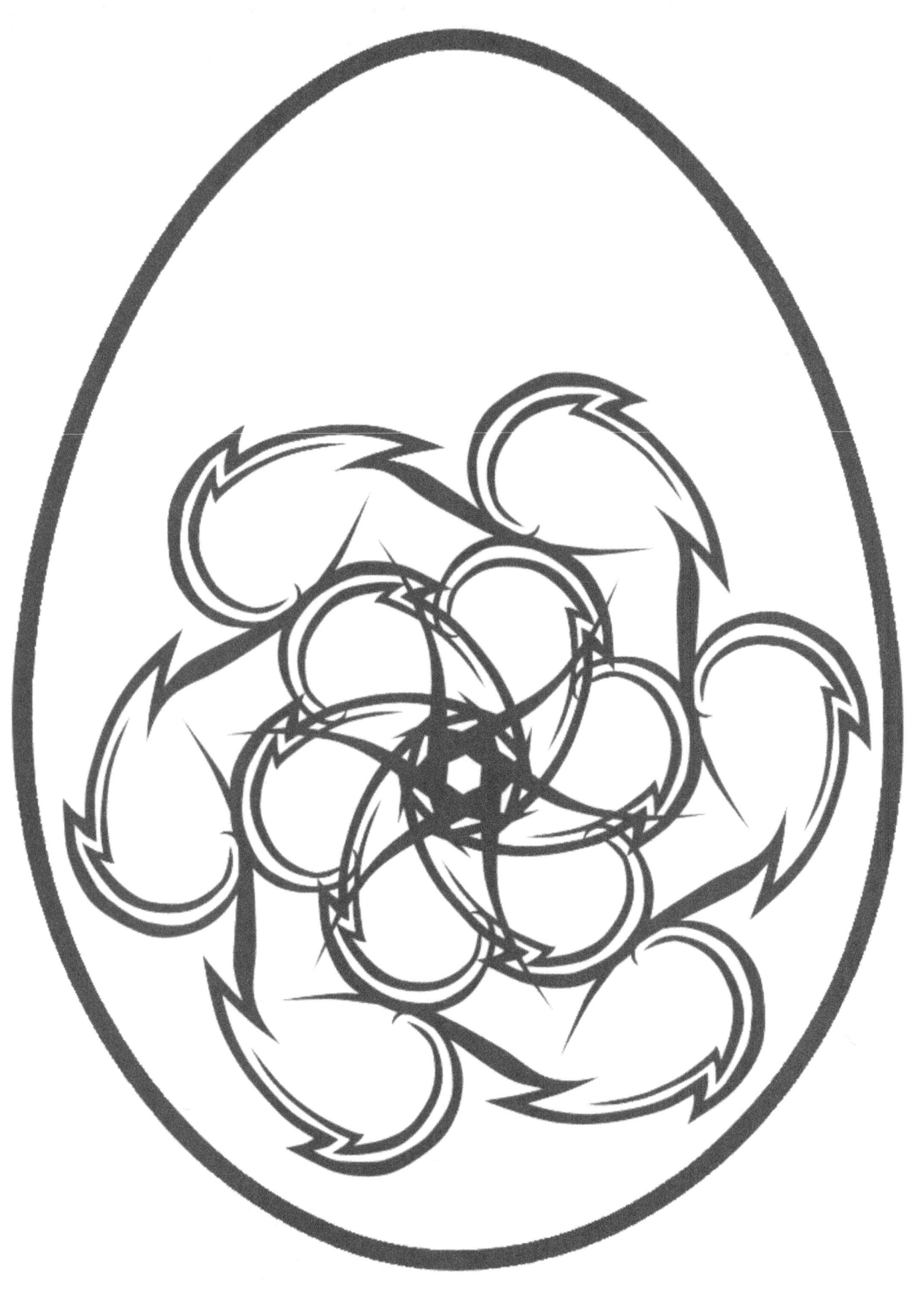